MANAGEMENT

TANTRA

Holistic Approaches to

Modern Leadership

Manoj Sam & Jay Kumar

ISBN: 978-1-7323740-7-2

Published by

INDUS NETWORK

Fort Myers, Florida 33913

yad yad ācharati śhreṣhṭhas
tat tad evetaro janaḥ
sa yat pramāṇaṁ kurute
lokas tad anuvartate

Bhagavad Gita (Chapter 3, Verse 21)

Translation: Whatever actions a great man performs, common men follow. And whatever standards he sets by exemplary acts, all the world pursues.

Meaning: Leaders set the standard through their actions. Their behavior and decisions influence others profoundly.

ā no bhadrāḥ kratavo yantu vishvataḥ
Rig Veda (Book 1, Hymn 34, Verse 7)

Let noble thoughts come to us from every side.

Meaning: A leader should encourage and embrace diverse perspectives and ideas for the benefit of all.

Management Tantra
Holistic Approaches to Modern Leadership

Introduction

"Tantra" in Management

Harmonizing Business and Human Potential

In the bustling heart of the corporate world, where bottom lines and quarterly reports dictate the rhythm of life, there existed a whisper—a subtle yet powerful idea that promised to revolutionize the very essence of management.

"Tantra," they called it.

At first glance, the word conjures images of ancient rituals and esoteric practices, far removed from the boardrooms and conference halls where decisions shape destinies. Yet, within the context of management, Tantra revealed itself as a beacon of holistic wisdom—a philosophy that dared to embrace the interconnectedness of all facets within an organization.

Imagine a CEO, weary from navigating the choppy waters of market competition, stumbling upon this concept like a lost explorer finding a hidden treasure. "Holistic," he mused, rolling the word around on his tongue as though testing its weight. It spoke of a perspective that transcended mere profit margins and shareholder satisfaction—a vision that acknowledged the intricate web linking strategy, culture, and human potential.

In the realm of Tantra in management, every decision, every policy, every initiative became a thread intricately woven into the fabric of a greater whole. It wasn't just about maximizing efficiency or minimizing costs; it was about nurturing an environment where every individual, from the janitor to the C-suite executive, could flourish.

Picture the HR manager, usually bound by spreadsheets and compliance protocols, suddenly awakening to the idea of transformative leadership. "Integrative," she whispered to herself, as though imparting a secret to the air around her. It was about weaving empathy into performance reviews, about seeing each employee not as a resource but as a person with aspirations and dreams.

And then, there was the finance director, renowned for his sharp analytical mind and cold, calculated decisions. Even he found himself drawn to the allure of Tantra in management. "Balance," he muttered, as he crunched numbers with renewed vigor. It wasn't enough to chase profits at any cost; true success lay in maintaining equilibrium between financial stability and ethical responsibility.

In the corridors of power, where ambitious visions collided with daily realities, Tantra in management emerged as a guiding philosophy—a roadmap to navigate the complexities of modern business with a compass that pointed not only to the north of profitability but also to the east of employee well-being, the south of sustainability, and the west of community impact.

For those who embraced it, Tantra in management became a journey—a journey of discovery and rediscovery, of learning to dance with the rhythm of change and finding harmony in diversity. It challenged leaders to see beyond the immediate gains and envision a future where success was measured not just in dollars and cents but in the richness of relationships forged and the legacy of positive impact left behind.

Tantra in management was not just a theory or a strategy; it was a call to embrace the full spectrum of human experience in pursuit of organizational excellence—a reminder that true transformation begins within, echoing outward to shape the world.

Key Principles:

1. **Holistic Perspective**: Unlike traditional management theories that often focus solely on profit and efficiency, Management Tantra adopts a holistic perspective. It acknowledges the interconnectedness of various facets within an organization—people, processes, culture, and environment—and seeks to balance these elements harmoniously for long-term prosperity.

2. **Integration of Mindfulness and Awareness**: Central to Management Tantra is the cultivation of mindfulness and awareness among leaders and employees alike. By fostering a deep understanding of the present moment and the dynamics at play within the organization, leaders can make informed decisions that align with broader strategic goals while remaining responsive to changing circumstances.

3. **Empowerment and Inclusivity**: Management Tantra promotes a culture of empowerment and inclusivity where every individual's unique talent and perspective are

valued. Leaders are encouraged to nurture a supportive environment that encourages innovation, creativity, and continuous learning, thereby harnessing the full potential of their teams.

4. **Ethical Governance and Sustainability**: Ethics and sustainability are fundamental tenets of Management Tantra. Leaders are called upon to make decisions that not only benefit the organization in the short term but also contribute positively to society and the environment in the long term. This ethical approach fosters trust among stakeholders and reinforces the organization's commitment to responsible corporate citizenship.

5. **Adaptability and Resilience**: In a rapidly changing global landscape, adaptability and resilience are crucial. Management Tantra encourages leaders to embrace change proactively, viewing challenges as opportunities for growth and innovation. By fostering a culture of resilience, organizations can navigate uncertainties more effectively and emerge stronger from adversity.

6. **Continuous Improvement and Learning**: Finally, Management Tantra advocates for a commitment to continuous improvement and learning at all levels of the organization. Leaders are encouraged to cultivate a growth mindset, promote knowledge-sharing initiatives, and invest in professional development opportunities that empower employees to evolve alongside the organization.

The Essence of Management Tantra

The CEO's Transformation

Sarah stood at the threshold of a challenge unlike any she had faced before. As she took the reins of a struggling company, the weight of responsibility settled on her shoulders. The once-thriving enterprise was now mired in financial woes, dwindling morale, and a culture overshadowed by distrust and uncertainty.

Her appointment as CEO came with a mandate for change. While the board emphasized the need for profitability and turnaround, Sarah knew that true transformation went beyond balance sheets and profit margins. She envisioned a company where success was measured not just in numbers but in the well-being and growth of its people.

From the outset, Sarah set out to redefine the company's priorities. Instead of imposing top-down directives focused solely on cutting costs and maximizing revenue, she began by listening.

She engaged with employees at all levels, seeking their insights and understanding their concerns.

Through these conversations, Sarah identified a critical need for a cultural shift. She recognized that employee well-being was the foundation upon which sustainable success could be built. She introduced comprehensive wellness programs aimed at promoting physical health, mental well-being, and work-life balance.

Sarah understood that investing in her team's professional development was essential to revitalizing the company. She implemented training initiatives that empowered employees to expand their skills and explore new opportunities within the organization. By fostering a culture of continuous learning and growth, Sarah inspired confidence and loyalty among her workforces.

Open communication became the cornerstone of Sarah's leadership philosophy. She encouraged transparency and honesty, ensuring that every employee felt valued and heard. Town hall meetings, feedback sessions, and regular updates became integral to fostering a sense of unity and purpose.

Transforming the company was not without its challenges. Sarah faced resistance from skeptics who questioned the feasibility of her approach. Some board members and investors were wary of her emphasis on employee well-being, fearing it would detract from the urgent need for financial recovery.

Yet, Sarah remained steadfast in her belief that a thriving workforce would drive sustainable profitability. She articulated a compelling vision for the future, illustrating how a culture of care and collaboration could yield innovative solutions and enhanced productivity.

Slowly but surely, Sarah's vision began to take root. Employee engagement soared as morale improved. Productivity metrics showed promising signs of growth, and the company's reputation as an employer of choice began to attract top talent from across the industry.

Under Sarah's leadership, the company not only recovered but thrived. Profits rebounded as operational efficiencies and innovation initiatives gained momentum. The once-failing enterprise became a model of success, celebrated not just for its financial performance but for its commitment to holistic growth and sustainable practices.

As Sarah reflected on her journey, she felt a deep sense of pride in what she had accomplished. The company was no longer just a place of work but a community where people thrived and dreams were realized. Her leadership had not only revitalized a failing enterprise but had also redefined what it meant to be a CEO.

Sarah's story serves as a testament to the transformative power of prioritizing employee well-being and holistic growth in corporate leadership. Her legacy inspires future generations of leaders to embrace a human-centered approach to business, where success is measured not just in profits but in the positive impact on people's lives.

As the sun set on another successful day for the company, Sarah looked to the horizon with optimism. The journey of transformation was ongoing, and she was determined to continue nurturing a culture where people and purpose flourished together.

Sarah's journey illustrates how a CEO's commitment to prioritizing employee well-being and fostering holistic growth can lead to the revitalization of a struggling company into a thriving, profitable enterprise. Her leadership exemplifies the transformative potential of investing in people as the cornerstone of sustainable business success.

Key Points:-

1. **Challenging Beginning**: Sarah takes over a struggling company burdened with financial issues, low morale, and a culture of distrust.

2. **Vision for Transformation**: Sarah believes in a holistic approach to transformation beyond just financial recovery. She emphasizes employee well-being, growth, and cultural change.

3. **Listening and Engagement**: Sarah starts by listening to employees at all levels, understanding their concerns, and involving them in the transformation process.

4. **Cultural Shift**: Recognizing the importance of employee well-being, Sarah introduces comprehensive wellness programs and emphasizes work-life balance.

5. **Investing in Development**: Sarah implements training initiatives to enhance skills and empower employees, fostering a culture of continuous learning and growth.

6. **Communication and Transparency**: Open communication becomes central to Sarah's leadership style, ensuring every employee feels valued and informed through town hall meetings and feedback sessions.

7. **Challenges and Resistance**: Sarah faces skepticism from board members and investors who doubt her focus on employee well-being over immediate financial recovery.

8. **Driving Sustainable Profitability**: Despite challenges, Sarah's approach leads to improved employee engagement, productivity, and profitability over time.

9. **Achievements**: Under Sarah's leadership, the company not only recovers but thrives, becoming a model of success known for its holistic growth and sustainable practices.

10. **Legacy and Inspiration**: Sarah's story inspires future leaders to prioritize people-centric approaches to business, showing that investing in employees can lead to sustainable business success.

11. **Ongoing Journey**: Sarah remains committed to nurturing a culture where people and purpose flourish, continuing to lead the company towards sustained growth and innovation.

Chapter 1.

The Foundation of Management Tantra

1.(a)

Holistic Leadership

The Enlightened Emperor

In the ancient land of Magadha, where kingdoms rose and fell like waves upon the shore, there emerged a prince named Ashoka. He was born into the Maurya dynasty, destined to inherit a vast empire that stretched from the Himalayas to the Deccan plateau.

From a young age, Ashoka showed promise as a warrior and leader. His father, King Bindusara, recognized his son's potential and groomed him for future rule. Under the tutelage of wise mentors and skilled generals, Ashoka learned the art of warfare and statecraft. He accompanied his father on campaigns across the subcontinent, witnessing firsthand the brutality of conquest and the cost of ambition.

As Ashoka grew older, his ambitions mirrored those of his father. He yearned to expand the Maurya empire, believing that conquest and expansion were the hallmarks of a great ruler. His campaigns were fierce and relentless, and he won many battles, each victory adding to his reputation as a formidable warrior.

Yet, amidst the glory of victory, Ashoka could not escape a growing sense of unease. He saw the devastation wrought by war—the cities razed, the fields plundered, and the people left homeless and destitute. Each conquest brought him further from the ideals of justice and compassion instilled in him by his mother and the teachings of his childhood.

One fateful day, during a campaign in the Kalinga region, Ashoka's life took a dramatic turn. The Battle of Kalinga was fierce and bloody, with thousands perishing on both sides. As Ashoka surveyed the aftermath—a landscape littered with bodies and the cries of the wounded echoing in his ears—he felt a profound sense of sorrow and remorse.

Among the ruins of a once-thriving city, Ashoka met a young girl named Sita, who had lost her family and home in the battle. Her tear-streaked face and trembling hands touched something deep within Ashoka's heart. He realized that his thirst for conquest had brought nothing but suffering and destruction to countless innocent lives.

That night, under the canopy of stars, Ashoka wrestled with his conscience. He sought solace in the teachings of Buddha, whose words of compassion and non-violence resonated with him. He vowed to change his ways and dedicate himself to a new path—

one of holistic leadership guided by empathy and understanding.

Upon returning to the capital city of Pataliputra, Ashoka embarked on a journey of transformation. He convened his council of advisors and announced sweeping reforms aimed at fostering peace and prosperity throughout the empire. He abolished harsh punishments and promoted laws that protected the rights of all citizens, regardless of caste or creed.

Ashoka's reforms extended beyond the realm of governance. He established hospitals and dispensaries to provide free medical care to the sick and injured. He built universities and monasteries where scholars and monks could study and propagate knowledge. He commissioned the construction of roads and rest houses to facilitate trade and travel across his vast empire.

But perhaps Ashoka's most enduring legacy was his commitment to spreading the teachings of dharma—the moral and ethical principles that guided his rule. He sent emissaries to neighboring kingdoms and beyond, carrying messages of peace and goodwill. He erected pillars and inscribed edicts throughout the empire, proclaiming his vision of a just and compassionate society.

As the years passed, Ashoka's empire flourished not only in wealth and power but in a profound sense of unity and harmony. The people revered him not only as a wise ruler but as a compassionate leader who had transformed their lives for the better. Under his benevolent rule, art and culture thrived, trade flourished, and the empire enjoyed a golden age of prosperity.

When Ashoka passed away, his legacy endured through the ages. His reign became a beacon of hope and inspiration for future generations of leaders, reminding them that true greatness lies not in conquest and glory, but in empathy, compassion, and the understanding that all beings are interconnected in the circle of life.

And so, the tale of Ashoka the Great, the enlightened emperor who embraced holistic leadership, continues to echo through history as a testament to the transformative power of compassion and wisdom in governance.

Key Points: -

Early Ambitions and Realizations:

➤ Ashoka initially embraced the traditional view that conquest and expansion were essential for greatness.

➤ He participated in campaigns and witnessed firsthand the brutal consequences of war.

1. **Turning Point - The Battle of Kalinga:**

➤ The pivotal moment occurred during the Battle of Kalinga, where the scale of suffering and devastation deeply affected Ashoka.

➤ Meeting Sita, a young victim of the war, stirred empathy and remorse within him.

2. **Transformation and Holistic Leadership**:

   ➢ After introspection and influenced by Buddhist teachings, Ashoka underwent a profound personal transformation.

   ➢ He abandoned aggressive expansionism and embraced a leadership style rooted in empathy, justice, and compassion.

3. **Reforms and Policies**:

   ➢ Ashoka enacted comprehensive reforms aimed at promoting peace and welfare within his empire.

   ➢ He abolished harsh punishments, ensured equal rights regardless of social status, and promoted humanitarian policies.

4. **Social and Cultural Contributions**:

   ➢ Beyond governance, Ashoka focused on societal well-being by establishing healthcare facilities, educational institutions, and infrastructure for trade and travel.

5. **Legacy and Enduring Impact**:

   ➢ Ashoka's reign ushered in a golden age marked by prosperity, cultural flourishing, and a sense of unity among his people.

➤ His commitment to dharma and compassionate governance left a lasting legacy that inspired future generations of leaders.

6. **Holistic Leadership Principles**:

➤ Ashoka demonstrated that true greatness in leadership lies not in conquest or power alone, but in empathy, ethical governance, and a holistic approach that considers the well-being of all citizens.

1.(b)

Mindfulness and Presence

The Mindful Executive

In the heart of the bustling metropolis, surrounded by towering skyscrapers and bustling streets, there stood the headquarters of Horizon Enterprises. At the top floor of the sleek glass tower, overlooking the city's skyline, John Hamilton, the CEO of Horizon, sat in his spacious corner office.

John had climbed the corporate ladder with determination and drive, earning a reputation for his sharp intellect and decisive leadership. Yet, amidst the high-pressure demands of running a multinational corporation, John often found himself overwhelmed by stress and the relentless pace of business.

One day, during a particularly hectic week filled with back-to-back meetings and looming deadlines, John paused to reflect on the toll that stress was taking on himself and his team. He noticed the tired faces of his colleagues, the tension in their voices, and the palpable sense of burnout that hung in the air.

That evening, as John sat in his office reviewing reports and emails, he came across an article on mindfulness and its benefits in the workplace. Intrigued, he delved deeper into the topic, reading about how mindfulness practices could reduce stress, enhance focus, and improve overall well-being.

Inspired by what he learned, John decided to take action. The next morning, during the weekly executive team meeting, he introduced a new initiative: daily mindfulness exercises for the entire leadership team. Some were skeptical at first, accustomed to the fast-paced, results-driven culture of the corporate world. But John, with his calm demeanor and persuasive arguments backed by research, convinced them to give it a try.

Under John's guidance, the executive team began incorporating mindfulness practices into their daily routine. Each morning before the start of their meetings, they gathered in a conference room with dimmed lights and soothing music. John led them through guided breathing exercises and mindfulness meditation, encouraging them to focus on the present moment and let go of distractions.

At first, it was challenging for some executives to quiet their racing thoughts and embrace stillness. But with John's patient guidance and gentle encouragement, they gradually began to experience the benefits of mindfulness. They noticed a sense of clarity and perspective emerging amidst the chaos of their demanding schedules. They learned to approach challenges with a calm mind and make decisions with greater insight.

As weeks turned into months, the impact of mindfulness on the executive team became evident. They became more attuned to each other's needs and perspectives, fostering a culture of open communication and collaboration. They found innovative solutions to complex problems, drawing on their enhanced creativity and resilience.

Moreover, the benefits extended beyond the executive suite. Teams throughout Horizon Enterprises started to adopt mindfulness practices, inspired by the positive changes they observed in their leaders. Employee engagement and satisfaction soared as stress levels decreased and productivity increased.

John himself underwent a transformation. He found renewed energy and enthusiasm for his work, balanced with a sense of calm and presence. He made time for regular mindfulness practices outside of work, incorporating yoga and nature walks into his routine to maintain his well-being.

As John reflected on the journey he and his team had taken, he felt a deep sense of fulfillment. The introduction of mindfulness had not only improved performance and productivity at Horizon Enterprises but had also enhanced the overall quality of life for everyone involved.

Under John's leadership, Horizon became known not only for its innovative business strategies but also for its commitment to holistic well-being and mindfulness in the workplace. Other companies looked to Horizon as a model of how mindfulness could transform organizational culture and enhance employee satisfaction.

And so, John Hamilton continued his journey as the mindful executive, guided by the belief that presence and mindfulness were not just tools for success in business but essential principles for living a fulfilling and balanced life. His legacy as a leader who prioritized the well-being of his team and fostered a culture of mindfulness continued to inspire others in the corporate world and beyond.

Key Points: -

1. **Recognition of Stress**: Despite his success, John and his team often experience stress and burnout due to the relentless pace of business.

2. **Discovery of Mindfulness**: During a hectic period, John discovers mindfulness through an article emphasizing its benefits in reducing stress, enhancing focus, and improving well-being.

3. **Initiative Implementation**: John introduces daily mindfulness exercises to his executive team despite initial skepticism, promoting calm and focus through guided practices like breathing exercises and meditation.

4. **Impact on Leadership**: Over time, executives experience improved clarity, perspective, and decision-making abilities. They foster a culture of open communication and collaboration.

5. **Organizational Impact**: Mindfulness practices spread throughout Horizon Enterprises, leading to reduced stress, increased productivity, and heightened employee satisfaction across teams.

6. **Personal Transformation**: John personally benefits from mindfulness, finding renewed energy and balance. He integrates mindfulness practices like yoga and nature walks into his routine.

7. **Leadership Legacy**: John's approach transforms Horizon Enterprises into a model of holistic well-being and mindfulness in the workplace, influencing other companies to adopt similar practices.

8. **Philosophy of Mindful Leadership**: John believes that mindfulness and presence are essential not only for business success but also for a fulfilling life, inspiring others with his balanced approach to leadership.

9. **Overall Impact**: Mindfulness becomes a cornerstone of Horizon's success story, showcasing how prioritizing well-being can enhance both organizational culture and performance.

Chapter 2.

The Art of Communication

2.(a)

Power of Authentic Communication

The Manager's Turnaround

In the heart of downtown Rivertown, nestled among the bustling streets and towering office buildings, there was a marketing firm known as Crestview Communications. At its helm was Maria Santos, a driven and ambitious manager who had risen through the ranks with her sharp wit and strategic acumen.

Maria's team at Crestview had once been a powerhouse of creativity and collaboration. They had launched successful campaigns, won prestigious awards, and garnered praise from clients and competitors alike. But over time, cracks began to appear in the team's cohesion. Miscommunications led to misunderstandings, cliques formed, and trust eroded.

One morning, as Maria walked through the open office layout, she couldn't ignore the palpable tension that hung in the air. She saw hushed conversations and strained smiles, a stark contrast to the vibrant and harmonious atmosphere that had once defined Crestview.

Concerned about the declining morale and productivity, Maria took a step back to reflect on what had gone wrong. She realized that the root of the problem lay in communication—or rather, the lack thereof. In the pursuit of results and efficiency, she had prioritized directives and deadlines over fostering genuine connections and open dialogue within her team.

Determined to initiate change, Maria embarked on a journey to rebuild trust through authentic communication. She started by scheduling one-on-one meetings with each team member, setting aside formalities to engage in candid conversations about their concerns, aspirations, and frustrations. She listened intently, acknowledging their perspectives and validating their experiences.

Armed with insights from her team members, Maria took decisive action to foster openness and transparency within Crestview. She implemented weekly team meetings where everyone was encouraged to share their thoughts, ideas, and challenges without fear of judgment. She emphasized the importance of active listening and respectful communication, setting a precedent for collaborative problem-solving.

To further cultivate trust, Maria introduced a practice of sharing successes and failures openly. She celebrated achievements and milestones, while also acknowledging setbacks as opportunities for growth and learning. This culture of transparency helped her team members feel valued and empowered, knowing that their contributions were recognized and appreciated.

As Maria's efforts to promote authentic communication gained momentum, she witnessed a remarkable transformation within Crestview. Team members began to collaborate more effectively, leveraging their diverse skills and perspectives to tackle complex projects and overcome obstacles together. The once-fractured team started to function as a cohesive unit once again, driven by a shared sense of purpose and mutual respect.

With open lines of communication, ideas flowed freely, innovation thrived, and productivity soared. Clients noticed the positive change in Crestview's approach and praised Maria for her leadership in nurturing a supportive and creative work environment.

As Maria reflected on the journey that had brought her team back from the brink, she realized the profound impact of authentic communication on organizational culture and success. By prioritizing transparency, openness, and genuine connection, she had not only rebuilt trust within her team but had also laid a foundation for sustained growth and resilience.

Maria's leadership at Crestview became a beacon of authenticity in the corporate world, inspiring other managers and organizations to prioritize genuine communication as a catalyst for positive change. Her legacy as the manager who turned around a fractured team through the power of authentic communication continued to resonate, reminding leaders everywhere of the transformative potential of fostering trust and collaboration within their teams.

Key Points: -

1. **Initial Success and Decline**: Crestview Communications, led by Maria Santos, initially thrived with creativity and collaboration, achieving success in campaigns and earning industry recognition.

2. **Communication Breakdown**: Over time, cracks in team cohesion emerged due to miscommunications, misunderstandings, and cliques, leading to decreased morale and productivity.

3. **Recognition of the Issue**: Maria observed the growing tension and realized that the lack of authentic communication was at the root of the team's problems.

4. **Initiating Change**: Maria took proactive steps to rebuild trust through authentic communication:

➢ Scheduled one-on-one meetings to listen to team members' concerns and aspirations.

➢ Introduced weekly team meetings to encourage open dialogue and idea-sharing.

> ➢ Emphasized active listening and respectful communication as crucial for collaboration.

5. **Cultural Transformation**: By fostering transparency and celebrating both successes and failures openly, Maria cultivated a culture where team members felt valued, empowered, and motivated.

6. **Positive Impact**: The transformation led to improved collaboration, innovation, and productivity within Crestview. Clients noticed the positive change and praised Maria's leadership.

7. **Reflecting on Success**: Maria realized the profound impact of authentic communication on organizational culture and success. It not only rebuilt trust but also laid a foundation for sustained growth and resilience.

8. **Inspiring Others**: Maria's approach became a model for other managers and organizations, highlighting the transformative potential of genuine communication in fostering trust and collaboration.

9. **Legacy**: Maria's leadership at Crestview left a legacy as a beacon of authenticity, inspiring leaders to prioritize genuine communication for positive organizational change.

2.(b)

Power of Active Listening

The HR Director's Resolution

In the corporate headquarters of Evergreen Industries, located in the heart of a bustling city, David Reynolds served as the Director of Human Resources. David was known for his diplomatic skills and calm demeanor, qualities that had earned him respect and admiration among his colleagues.

However, one fateful Monday morning, as David stepped into his office, he sensed an unusual tension lingering in the air. Rumors of discontent among the finance and marketing teams had reached his ears over the weekend, but he hadn't anticipated the depth of the conflict that awaited him.

As David delved deeper into the situation, he discovered that the conflict stemmed from a recent reorganization that had led to overlapping responsibilities and unclear reporting structures between the two departments. Miscommunication and misunderstandings had escalated into animosity and resentment, threatening to undermine productivity and morale.

Determined to resolve the conflict swiftly and effectively, David scheduled a meeting with key stakeholders from both teams. He approached the situation with a commitment to practicing active listening—a technique he had learned early in his career and honed throughout his years as an HR professional.

During the meeting, David set aside his own agenda and focused wholeheartedly on understanding the perspectives and concerns of each team member. He employed techniques of active listening, such as maintaining eye contact, nodding to show understanding, and paraphrasing to ensure clarity.

As team members shared their frustrations and grievances, David listened attentively, probing deeper to uncover the root causes of the conflict. He refrained from interrupting or passing judgment, creating a safe space where individuals felt heard and respected.

Through active listening, David gained valuable insights into the underlying issues that had fueled the tension between the finance and marketing teams. He discovered that the conflict was not merely about overlapping responsibilities but also about communication breakdowns, perceived biases, and unresolved misunderstandings dating back several months.

Armed with this understanding, David facilitated an open dialogue where team members expressed their ideas for resolving the conflict constructively. He encouraged brainstorming and collaboration, guiding them towards consensus on clear roles, responsibilities, and communication protocols moving forward.

Through David's commitment to active listening and effective facilitation, the finance and marketing teams reached a resolution that addressed their concerns and restored harmony. They developed a comprehensive action plan that clarified roles, improved communication channels, and established regular check-ins to monitor progress and address emerging issues proactively.

The atmosphere at Evergreen Industries shifted from tension to cooperation, as team members embraced a newfound spirit of collaboration and mutual respect. Productivity soared, and morale improved significantly, setting a positive tone for future endeavors within the company.

David's success in resolving the conflict through active listening garnered praise and recognition from senior management and colleagues alike. His approach became a model for effective conflict resolution and communication within Evergreen Industries and beyond.

Inspired by his experience, David continued to advocate for active listening as a core competency in leadership and HR management. He conducted workshops and training sessions to empower managers and employees with the skills to listen deeply, understand perspectives, and foster positive relationships in the workplace.

As David reflected on the journey that had led to the resolution, he realized the transformative power of active listening in fostering understanding, building trust, and driving organizational success. His legacy as the HR Director who resolved a major conflict through the art of active listening continued to inspire others to embrace this fundamental skill in their professional and personal interactions.

key Points: -

1. **Setting**: David Reynolds, HR Director at Evergreen Industries, known for his diplomatic skills, faces escalating conflict between finance and marketing teams due to recent reorganization.

2. **Conflict Discovery**: Miscommunication and unclear responsibilities lead to animosity and productivity issues between the two departments.

3. **Approach**: David resolves to use active listening as a primary tool for conflict resolution, setting aside his own agenda to focus on understanding each team member's perspective.

4. **Active Listening Techniques**: During meetings, David maintains eye contact, nods to show understanding, and paraphrases to clarify and ensure all concerns are heard.

5. **Insight Gathering**: Through active listening, David uncovers underlying issues beyond overlapping

responsibilities, including communication breakdowns, biases, and unresolved misunderstandings.

6. **Facilitation of Dialogue**: David creates a safe space for open dialogue where team members collaboratively develop solutions to address grievances and improve communication.

7. **Resolution and Action Plan**: The teams reach consensus on clear roles, responsibilities, and communication protocols, developing an action plan with regular check-ins to ensure ongoing clarity and progress.

8. **Transformation**: Evergreen Industries' atmosphere shifts from tension to cooperation, boosting productivity and morale as teams embrace collaboration and mutual respect.

9. **Recognition and Legacy**: David's success in resolving the conflict through active listening earns praise from senior management, making his approach a model for effective conflict resolution and communication.

10. **Advocacy and Training**: Inspired by his experience, David promotes active listening through workshops and training, emphasizing its role in fostering understanding, trust, and organizational success.

11. **Reflection**: David recognizes the transformative power of active listening in professional interactions, underscoring its impact on building relationships and achieving positive outcomes.

Chapter 3.

The Art of Communication

3.(a)

Adaptive Thinking

The Startup Pivot

In the vibrant tech hub of Silicon Valley, where innovation thrived amidst the fast-paced energy of startups and venture capitalists, Emily Campbell embarked on her entrepreneurial journey. Armed with a vision and a passion for solving a pressing problem in the healthcare industry, Emily founded MedTech Solutions—a startup dedicated to revolutionizing patient care through technology.

Emily's journey began with boundless optimism and determination. She assembled a talented team of engineers, designers, and healthcare professionals who shared her vision. Together, they developed a groundbreaking mobile app designed to streamline patient-doctor communication and improve medical record management.

After months of tireless development and testing, MedTech Solutions launched its app to great anticipation. Emily and her team believed they had created a game-changer—a tool that would empower patients and healthcare providers alike, enhancing efficiency and quality of care.

However, reality soon set in as they faced the harsh truths of the market. Initial user feedback revealed challenges with usability and integration into existing healthcare systems. Healthcare providers expressed concerns about data security and compliance with regulatory standards. Meanwhile, potential investors hesitated, citing uncertainties in scalability and market adoption.

Instead of being discouraged, Emily saw an opportunity to pivot—a chance to adapt her business model based on market feedback and emerging trends. She embraced flexibility and agility, qualities she knew were crucial in navigating the rapidly changing landscape of the healthcare technology sector.

Emily convened her team for a series of brainstorming sessions and customer feedback interviews. They listened attentively to the pain points and suggestions voiced by healthcare providers, patients, and industry experts. This process of adaptive thinking led them to uncover new insights and identify areas where the app could be refined and enhanced.

Armed with a deeper understanding of their target users and market dynamics, Emily made the bold decision to pivot MedTech Solutions' business model. They shifted their focus from a standalone app to developing a cloud-based platform that integrated seamlessly with existing electronic health record systems. This pivot not only addressed concerns about data security and regulatory compliance but also positioned them as a strategic partner for healthcare providers seeking digital transformation.

Emily and her team worked tirelessly to iterate on their product, incorporating new features and functionalities based on iterative testing and user feedback. They forged partnerships with healthcare institutions and industry leaders, demonstrating the platform's value in improving patient outcomes and operational efficiency.

As Emily's adaptive thinking bore fruit, MedTech Solutions began to gain traction in the market. Healthcare providers embraced the platform for its user-friendly interface, robust security measures, and ability to streamline workflows. Patient engagement increased, and healthcare outcomes improved as providers gained real-time insights into patient data and treatment plans.

Investors took notice of MedTech Solutions' success story, impressed by Emily's leadership and the team's ability to pivot effectively in response to market demands. Funding rounds secured capital for further expansion and development, fueling innovation and scaling operations to reach more healthcare providers and patients nationwide.

As MedTech Solutions continued to grow and evolve, Emily reflected on the transformative power of adaptive thinking in entrepreneurship. She understood that success wasn't just about having a brilliant idea—it was about listening, learning, and being willing to pivot when necessary. Flexibility and adaptability had been their guiding principles, enabling them to navigate challenges and seize opportunities in a competitive industry.

Emily's journey as a startup founder who successfully pivoted her business model served as inspiration for aspiring entrepreneurs and innovators. Her story underscored the importance of embracing change, staying resilient in the face of adversity, and always prioritizing the needs of customers and stakeholders.

And so, Emily Campbell and MedTech Solutions continued their journey, driven by a commitment to transforming healthcare through adaptive thinking, innovation, and a steadfast belief in the power of technology to make a positive impact on people's lives.

key Points:

1. **Entrepreneurial Vision**: Emily Campbell founded MedTech Solutions in Silicon Valley to innovate healthcare through technology, aiming to improve patient care with a mobile app.

2. **Initial Challenges**: Despite optimism, the app faced usability issues, integration challenges with existing systems, and concerns over data security and regulatory compliance.

3. **Embracing Adaptation**: Rather than being discouraged, Emily embraced adaptive thinking, recognizing the need to pivot the business model based on market feedback and emerging trends.

4. **Iterative Approach**: Emily and her team conducted brainstorming sessions and customer interviews to refine the app, focusing on improving usability and addressing healthcare providers' concerns.

5. **Strategic Pivot**: They pivoted from a standalone app to a cloud-based platform integrated with electronic health record systems, enhancing security and compliance while positioning as a digital transformation partner for healthcare providers.

6. **Market Success**: The refined platform gained traction due to its user-friendly interface, robust security measures, and efficiency improvements in healthcare operations.

7. **Recognition and Growth**: Investors were impressed by the team's adaptive strategy, leading to successful funding rounds that fueled expansion and further product development.

8. **Lessons Learned**: Emily's journey underscored the importance of flexibility, resilience, and customer-centricity in entrepreneurship, emphasizing the transformative power of adaptive thinking.

9. **Inspiration and Impact**: Emily's success story inspired aspiring entrepreneurs, highlighting the importance of embracing change and prioritizing customer needs in building sustainable businesses.

10. **Continued Innovation**: MedTech Solutions continues to evolve under Emily's leadership, committed to leveraging technology for positive impacts on healthcare through continuous adaptation and innovation.

3.(b)

Fostering a Culture of Innovation

The Innovative Tech Company

In the heart of Silicon Valley, nestled among the giants of technology, stood Tech Pearl Solutions—a company renowned not only for its cutting-edge products but also for its relentless pursuit of innovation. At its helm was CEO Rachel Hayes, a visionary leader known for fostering a culture where creativity thrived and bold ideas were not just encouraged but celebrated.

Tech Pearl Solutions had humble beginnings. Founded by a group of ambitious engineers fresh out of college, the company started in a garage with dreams as big as the valley itself. What set them apart from the start was their unwavering belief in the power of innovation. Every Friday evening, they gathered around a whiteboard, brainstorming ideas that ranged from the practical to the fantastical.

Rachel Hayes joined the company during its early days, bringing with her a fervent passion for technology and a keen eye for untapped potential. She understood that to succeed in the ever-evolving tech landscape, they needed more than just great ideas—they needed a culture that nurtured innovation at its core.

Under Rachel's leadership, Tech Pearl Solutions became a beacon for creative thinkers. The office walls were adorned with murals depicting scenes from science fiction, a constant reminder that the future they were building was limited only by their imagination. Teams were given the freedom to explore new technologies and experiment with unconventional approaches, knowing that failure was not frowned upon but seen as a stepping stone to success.

The company invested heavily in workshops and seminars that encouraged cross-disciplinary collaboration. Engineers rubbed shoulders with artists, data scientists with psychologists, each exchange sparking new ideas and pushing boundaries further. Rachel herself often walked the halls, engaging in impromptu discussions with employees at all levels, always on the lookout for that next breakthrough concept.

It wasn't long before Tech Pearl Solutions began making headlines. Their flagship product, EchoSphere, a revolutionary AI-powered virtual assistant, was hailed as a game-changer in the industry. What the public didn't see were the countless late-night coding sessions, the heated debates over algorithm optimization, and the moments of doubt that were overcome through sheer perseverance and belief in their vision.

Behind every success was a team emboldened by a culture that valued risk-taking and innovation. Employees were given the autonomy to pursue passion projects, with dedicated resources allocated to support even the most unconventional ideas. The company's annual innovation fair became a showcase of ingenuity, where prototypes and proof-of-concepts vied for attention, each one a testament to the power of creativity unleashed.

As Tech Pearl Solutions continued to grow, so did the challenges they faced. Competitors emerged, each one eager to replicate their success. The pressure to innovate became even greater, yet Rachel remained steadfast in her belief that true innovation could not be rushed or forced. She encouraged her team to take calculated risks, to think beyond the confines of conventional wisdom, and to never lose sight of the human impact their technology could have.

The company expanded its reach, opening offices in global tech hubs from Tokyo to London. Each new location brought fresh perspectives and cultural diversity, enriching their creative ecosystem even further. Rachel's leadership style, characterized by empathy and a genuine passion for fostering talent, earned her the loyalty and admiration of employees worldwide.

Tech Pearl Solutions stands as a testament to what can be achieved when innovation is more than just a buzzword—it's a way of life. Rachel Hayes, now a revered figure in the tech industry, continues to champion the next generation of innovators. The company's commitment to fostering creativity and empowering its employees remains as strong as ever, ensuring that the spirit of innovation will continue to thrive for years to come.

In a world where change is the only constant, Tech Pearl Solutions remains at the forefront, pushing boundaries and redefining what's possible. The journey has been one of triumphs and setbacks, of moments of inspiration and hard-won victories. But through it all, one thing remains clear: the pursuit of innovation is not just about creating groundbreaking products— it's about shaping a better future for all.

As the sun sets over Silicon Valley, casting a golden hue over the Tech Pearl Solutions headquarters, Rachel Hayes stands on the rooftop terrace, gazing out at the skyline that has witnessed their journey from humble beginnings to global prominence. The spirit of innovation that brought them here still burns bright, a beacon of hope and possibility for generations of dreamers yet to come.

And as she takes a deep breath, Rachel smiles, knowing that the greatest innovations are yet to be imagined, waiting to be discovered by those bold enough to dream.

key Points: -

1. **Founding and Vision**: Tech Pearl Solutions started in Silicon Valley, founded by ambitious engineers in a garage. They believed in the power of innovation from the outset, gathering weekly to brainstorm ideas.

2. **Leadership of Rachel Hayes**: CEO Rachel Hayes joined early, bringing a passion for technology and a focus on nurturing innovation. She cultivated a culture where creativity flourished, and bold ideas were celebrated.

3. **Cultural Environment**: The office culture was marked by murals of science fiction scenes, symbolizing limitless possibilities. Teams had freedom to explore new technologies and unconventional approaches, with failure seen as a path to success.

4. **Cross-Disciplinary Collaboration**: The company invested in workshops that encouraged collaboration across disciplines (engineers, artists, data scientists, psychologists). This fostered new ideas and pushed boundaries.

5. **Breakthroughs and Innovations**: EchoSphere, their flagship AI-powered virtual assistant, was a breakthrough product that garnered industry acclaim. Success was built on late-night coding sessions, debates, and perseverance.

6. **Empowerment and Autonomy**: Employees were empowered to pursue passion projects with dedicated resources. An annual innovation fair showcased prototypes, highlighting the company's commitment to creativity.

7. **Global Expansion and Challenges**: As Tech Pearl grew, so did competition. Rachel emphasized the importance of calculated risks and maintaining a focus on human impact amidst global expansion.

8. **Leadership Style**: Rachel's empathetic leadership style earned her global respect. She championed talent development and remained committed to fostering a culture of innovation.

9. **Legacy and Future**: Tech Pearl Solutions stands as a testament to innovation as a way of life. Rachel Hayes continues to inspire future innovators, confident that the spirit of innovation will endure.

10. **Vision for the Future**: The narrative concludes with Rachel Hayes looking towards the future, optimistic that the greatest innovations are yet to be discovered, driven by bold dreams and perseverance.

Chapter 4.

The Art of Communication

4.(a)

Servant Leadership

A Recipe for Success

Nestled in a bustling corner of downtown, where the aroma of freshly baked bread mingled with the tantalizing scent of spices, stood a quaint yet vibrant restaurant named "Harmony Kitchen." It was here that Alex Rivera found himself as the newly appointed restaurant manager, ready to embark on a journey that would not only transform the business but also redefine his approach to leadership.

Alex had always been passionate about hospitality. From a young age, he found joy in bringing people together through food and creating memorable dining experiences. When he took over as the manager of Harmony Kitchen, however, he faced a daunting challenge. The restaurant was struggling—dwindling customer satisfaction, high turnover rates among staff, and a general sense of disconnection among the team.

Instead of diving headfirst into implementing new policies or cutting costs, Alex decided to take a step back. He spent hours observing his team, listening to their concerns, and understanding their aspirations. What he discovered was a group of talented individuals who were passionate about their work but felt undervalued and unheard.

Armed with a newfound understanding of his team's needs, Alex set out to create a culture of trust and collaboration. He started small, implementing weekly team meetings where everyone had a chance to voice their ideas and concerns. He encouraged open communication and genuine feedback, fostering an environment where every team member felt valued and respected.

Alex also prioritized professional development, organizing workshops and training sessions to enhance their skills and build their confidence. He recognized and celebrated their achievements, no matter how small, reinforcing a sense of pride and ownership among the staff.

As morale improved, so did the atmosphere in the restaurant. Customers noticed the change—a warmer welcome, attentive service, and a genuine eagerness to ensure every dining experience was exceptional. Word of mouth spread, bringing back old patrons and attracting new ones curious to experience the revitalized Harmony Kitchen.

Despite the initial success, Alex faced challenges along the way. The restaurant industry was unforgiving, with fluctuating customer preferences and economic pressures. There were times when profits dipped, and morale wavered. Yet, Alex remained steadfast in his commitment to servant leadership.

During tough times, he rolled up his sleeves alongside his team, never asking them to do anything he wouldn't do himself. He encouraged a sense of camaraderie and unity, reminding everyone that they were in it together. His transparency and humility in addressing challenges earned him the loyalty and dedication of his team, who rallied behind him with unwavering support.

As Harmony Kitchen flourished under Alex's leadership, his approach to servant leadership began to influence others in the industry. Competing restaurants took note of the positive changes—a renewed focus on employee well-being, a shift towards empowering frontline staff, and a deeper understanding of the symbiotic relationship between employee satisfaction and customer experience.

Alex became a sought-after speaker at industry conferences, where he shared his journey and the transformative power of servant leadership. He emphasized that true leadership wasn't about wielding authority or demanding obedience but about serving others selflessly, empowering them to reach their full potential.

Harmony Kitchen stands not just as a successful restaurant but as a beacon of servant leadership in the hospitality industry. Under Alex's guidance, the restaurant not only regained its place in the hearts of the community but also became a model of excellence and compassion.

Alex Rivera, now revered not only as a manager but as a mentor and advocate for servant leadership, continues to inspire others to lead with humility and empathy. His journey with Harmony Kitchen serves as a reminder that by prioritizing the needs of others, we not only foster a thriving work environment but also create lasting impacts that extend far beyond the walls of any restaurant.

As Alex stands in the doorway of Harmony Kitchen, watching satisfied patrons linger over their meals and staff members bustling with energy, he reflects on the journey that brought him here. The lessons he learned—of listening deeply, leading with compassion, and believing in the potential of every individual—have shaped not just his career but his entire outlook on life.

And as he looks forward, Alex knows that the principles of servant leadership he embraced will continue to guide him, paving the way for new opportunities to make a difference and inspire others to do the same.

Key Points: -

1. **Introduction to Harmony Kitchen**: Alex Rivera becomes the manager of Harmony Kitchen, a struggling restaurant known for its disconnection among staff and dwindling customer satisfaction.

2. **Alex's Approach to Leadership**: Instead of immediate changes, Alex observes and listens to his team, understanding their concerns and aspirations.

3. **Creating a Culture of Trust**: Alex initiates weekly team meetings for open communication and encourages genuine feedback. He values every team member and fosters a sense of respect and collaboration.

4. **Focus on Professional Development**: Alex organizes workshops and training sessions to enhance skills and boost team confidence. He celebrates team achievements, reinforcing pride and ownership.

5. **Impact on Morale and Customer Experience**: As morale improves, so does customer satisfaction. Harmony Kitchen gains a reputation for attentive service and exceptional dining experiences.

6. **Challenges and Resilience**: Despite challenges like fluctuating customer preferences and economic pressures, Alex maintains his commitment to servant

leadership, working alongside his team with humility and transparency.

7. **Influence in the Industry**: Alex's approach influences other restaurants, sparking a shift towards employee well-being and empowering frontline staff. He becomes a respected speaker on servant leadership.

8. **Legacy of Harmony Kitchen**: Under Alex's leadership, Harmony Kitchen becomes a model of servant leadership in the hospitality industry, known for excellence and compassion.

9. **Alex Rivera's Journey**: Alex evolves from a manager to a mentor and advocate for servant leadership, inspiring others with his humility, empathy, and belief in individual potential.

10. **Future Outlook**: Alex sees servant leadership as a guiding principle for making a lasting difference, both in his career and personal life, continuing to inspire others.

4.(b)

Building High Performance Teams

The Champions Coach

In the heart of a small town nestled between rolling hills and whispering forests, Coach Benjamin Smith stood as a pillar of inspiration and leadership. For decades, he had dedicated his life to the game he loved and the young athletes who passed through his care. His legacy, however, was not just in the victories on the field but in the bonds of unity and resilience he forged among his teams.

Coach Smith's journey began on a crisp autumn morning, when he first set foot on the weathered turf of Greenfield High School's football field. Fresh out of college, armed with dreams of coaching greatness, he was greeted by a team of spirited but disjointed players. Each possessed raw talent, yet they lacked the cohesion needed to excel as a unit.

Rather than imposing strict rules or focusing solely on strategy, Coach Smith took a different approach. He spent hours observing his players, learning their strengths and weaknesses, and understanding their individual aspirations. What he saw was a mosaic of potential waiting to be shaped into something greater.

Armed with insights gleaned from his observations, Coach Smith set about nurturing a culture of trust and respect among his team. He emphasized the importance of communication, both on and off the field, encouraging players to support one another and collaborate towards a common goal. He instilled a sense of pride in the team's identity, fostering a belief that they were stronger together than they could ever be alone.

Recognizing that each player brought something unique to the table, Coach Smith tailored his coaching approach accordingly. He celebrated their individual strengths, whether it was a quarterback's precision passing or a lineman's unwavering determination. By empowering each player to shine in their own way, he cultivated a team dynamic where every member felt valued and essential to the collective success.

The road to championship glory was not without its challenges. There were setbacks—a crushing defeat that tested their resolve, injuries that threatened to derail their season, and moments of doubt that crept into their minds. Yet, Coach Smith remained a steady presence, guiding his team through adversity with unwavering faith and determination.

He taught them the importance of resilience, of bouncing back stronger after every setback. He fostered a spirit of accountability, where players held themselves and each other to the highest standards of excellence. And through it all, he never lost sight of the values that anchored their journey—integrity, perseverance, and the unbreakable bond of brotherhood forged through shared sacrifice.

As the season unfolded, Coach Smith's vision began to bear fruit. The once-disparate group of individuals had transformed into a cohesive, high-performing team. They moved with synchronized precision on the field, anticipating each other's moves instinctively. Off the field, they stood united, a band of brothers bound by a common purpose and unwavering belief in their ability to achieve greatness.

Their journey culminated in a championship game that would go down in school history. Against all odds, they emerged victorious, their triumph a testament to the power of teamwork, leadership, and unwavering dedication. The community erupted in jubilation, celebrating not just a trophy but the spirit of resilience and unity that Coach Smith had instilled in his team.

Coach Benjamin Smith stands on the sidelines, a proud smile on his weathered face. The lessons he imparted to his players—of embracing diversity, leveraging individual strengths, and trusting in the power of teamwork—have left an indelible mark on their lives.

Years later, former players gather to reminisce about their time under Coach Smith's guidance. They speak of the lessons learned—the importance of humility in victory, the resilience in defeat, and the enduring bonds of friendship forged through shared triumphs and hardships. They credit Coach Smith not just for their success on the field but for shaping them into the leaders, mentors, and role models they would become in their own right.

And as Coach Smith watches his players embark on their own journeys, he knows that the true measure of his success lies not in the trophies won or records broken, but in the lives touched and the legacies of leadership carried forward.

In the quiet of his study, surrounded by mementos of a storied coaching career, Coach Benjamin Smith reflects on the journey that brought him here. His passion for the game, his unwavering belief in the potential of every player, and his commitment to building high-performance teams have defined his legacy.

As the sun sets over Greenfield, casting a golden glow over the fields where dreams were realized and bonds were forged, Coach Smith closes his eyes with a heart full of gratitude. For In the end, it was not just about winning games—it was about empowering others to discover their own greatness and inspiring them to reach new heights, both on and off the field.

key Points: -

1. **Introduction of Coach Benjamin Smith:**

   ➤ Coach Smith is portrayed as a central figure in a small town, dedicated to coaching and inspiring young athletes.

   ➤ His legacy is noted for emphasizing unity and resilience among his teams, not just achieving victories.

2. **Early Days at Greenfield High School:**

   ➤ Coach Smith's coaching journey began with a team of talented but disjointed players.

   ➤ Instead of strict rules, he focused on understanding each player's strengths and aspirations.

3. **Building a Culture of Trust and Respect:**

   ➤ He nurtured a culture where communication and collaboration were key.

   ➤ Emphasized pride in the team's identity and the strength of unity over individual efforts.

4. **Empowerment of Individual Strengths:**

➢ Celebrated and empowered each player's unique abilities, fostering a sense of value and contribution.

➢ Cultivated a team dynamic where every member felt essential to the team's success.

5. **Navigating Challenges and Adversity:**

➢ Despite setbacks like defeats, injuries, and doubts, Coach Smith remained a steadfast leader.

➢ Taught resilience, accountability, and upheld values like integrity and perseverance.

6. **Transformation into a Cohesive Team:**

➢ Over time, the team evolved into a synchronized, high-performing unit both on and off the field.

➢ United by a common purpose and belief in their collective potential.

7. **Culmination in Championship Victory:**

➢ Their journey led to a historic championship win, symbolizing the power of teamwork and dedication.

➢ The community celebrated not just their victory but the resilience and unity instilled by Coach Smith.

8. **Legacy and Reflections**:

> ➤ Coach Smith's teachings left a lasting impact on his players, influencing their lives beyond sports.

> ➤ Former players credit him for shaping them into leaders and role models.

9. **Measure of Success**:

> ➤ Coach Smith reflects on his career with gratitude, focusing on the personal growth and leadership legacies of his players.

> ➤ Emphasizes that true success lies in inspiring others to achieve greatness in all aspects of life.

Chapter 5.

The Art of Communication

5.(a)

Visionary Thinking

The NGO Leader

In the heart of bustling Nairobi, amidst the ebb and flow of humanity, Amina stood steadfast. Her eyes, a reflection of the verdant hills that cradled her childhood, bore witness to the struggles and dreams of her people. A teacher by profession, she had felt the pulse of societal inequities and the silent cries of neglected communities. But it was the day she witnessed the despair in the eyes of orphaned children that stirred something profound within her.

She founded Horizon of Hope, an NGO committed to lifting these children from the abyss of destitution. With each brick laid for a new school, each meal served to hungry mouths, Amina's resolve deepened. Yet, the challenges grew in tandem with her ambitions. Funds were scarce, bureaucracy stifling, and skepticism pervasive.

One sultry afternoon, under the acacia tree that shaded her makeshift office, Amina had an epiphany. It wasn't enough to mend wounds one child at a time. She needed to ignite a movement, a symphony of compassion and action that resonated across borders. She needed a vision that could stir the hearts of strangers into champions of change.

With relentless zeal, Amina articulated her vision: "Education without borders. Every child, regardless of circumstance, deserves a future illuminated by knowledge and hope."

Her words were like sparks in the dry savannah, igniting minds and hearts previously untouched by the plight of distant lands. News of her mission spread through the veins of the internet, reaching corners of the globe where empathy lay dormant. Donations trickled in, then poured. Volunteers arrived, not just from nearby villages but from continents away.

But visionary thinking does not shield from adversity. Amina navigated through storms of doubt and logistical nightmares. The bureaucracy that once stifled her now seemed insurmountable. Yet, with each setback, Amina found new wellsprings of resilience. Her team, once a motley crew of believers, now stood as a formidable force of change-makers.

Together, they built bridges where others saw chasms. They persevered through the darkest nights of doubt, illuminated only by the flickering hope of a child's smile. And in those moments of triumph—when a new school opened its doors, when a community tasted clean water for the first time—the world bore witness to the power of visionary thinking.

Years passed like fleeting seasons, leaving in their wake a legacy etched in the hearts of those touched by Horizon of Hope. Amina's vision had transcended the confines of mere charity. It had become a beacon, guiding lost souls towards a future where opportunity was not a privilege but a birthright.

As Amina stood before a gathering of global leaders, her voice resonated with the echoes of generations yet unborn. "Visionary thinking," she declared, "is not about dreaming in isolation. It is about summoning the collective conscience of humanity to envision a world where every child's potential is nurtured, regardless of circumstance."

And as she looked into the eyes of the next generation of leaders, she saw the spark of possibility flicker anew. For Amina knew that while her journey had been one of profound impact, the true measure of her vision lay in those who would carry it forward—each a testament to the enduring power of a clear and compelling vision.

In the quiet twilight of her years, Amina sat beneath the acacia tree, the same tree where she had once dreamed of a better tomorrow. Around her, the laughter of children echoed through the air, mingling with the hum of a bustling schoolyard. The vision she had dared to conceive had become a reality—one that transcended her lifetime and illuminated the path for generations to come.

And as the sun dipped below the horizon, casting a golden glow upon the savannah, Amina closed her eyes with a smile. For in her heart, she knew that visionary thinking had the power to ignite not just dreams, but destinies. And hers had been a life well-lived, guided by the unwavering belief that where there is vision, there is always hope.

key Points: -

1. **Origins and Inspiration**:

➢ Amina, a teacher in Nairobi, founded Horizon of Hope after witnessing the despair of orphaned children.

➢ Her childhood in the verdant hills instilled in her a deep empathy for societal inequities and neglected communities.

2. **Mission and Commitment**:

➢ Horizon of Hope aimed to lift children from destitution through education and basic needs provision.

➢ Amina's resolve strengthened despite challenges like scarce funds, bureaucratic hurdles, and skepticism.

3. **Epiphany and Vision**:

> ➤ Under an acacia tree, Amina realized the need for a broader vision beyond immediate charity work.

> ➤ She articulated a vision of "Education without borders," advocating for every child's right to knowledge and hope.

4. **Impact and Growth**:

> ➤ Amina's visionary thinking sparked a global movement, attracting donations and volunteers worldwide.

> ➤ Her team grew from a small group to a powerful force, overcoming obstacles and transforming communities.

5. **Triumphs and Challenges**:

> ➤ Despite adversity, Amina and her team persevered, building schools and providing clean water to communities.

> ➤ Their successes demonstrated the transformative power of visionary thinking in humanitarian efforts.

6. **Legacy and Future**:

> ➤ Over years, Amina's vision became a beacon of hope, leaving a lasting impact on countless lives.

> ➤ She emphasized that visionary thinking extends beyond personal dreams to inspire collective action and change.

7. **Reflection and Fulfillment**:

➤ In her later years, Amina saw her vision fulfilled as children laughed and learned under Horizon of Hope's initiatives.

➤ Her journey affirmed that visionary thinking can shape destinies and inspire future generations to continue her legacy.

5.(b)

Strategic Planning and Execution

Beyond Blueprints

In the bustling heart of Mumbai, amidst the cacophony of honking horns and hurried footsteps, Raj stood at the threshold of his latest challenge. As a seasoned project manager, he had weathered storms of uncertainty and navigated through the maze of intricate timelines. Yet, the project before him posed a unique test—a high-stakes endeavor that promised to redefine standards and expectations.

The boardroom hummed with anticipation as Raj outlined the blueprint for success. His words, a tapestry woven with precision and foresight, painted a picture of seamless collaboration and unwavering commitment to excellence. But beyond the glossy presentations and optimistic projections lay the gritty reality of execution—a terrain fraught with pitfalls and unforeseen obstacles.

For Raj, strategic planning was not just a preliminary exercise but a compass that guided every decision and action. With his team—a mosaic of talents and temperaments—he embarked on a journey fueled by clarity of purpose and unwavering determination. Meetings became crucibles of innovation, where ideas clashed and fused into strategies that promised to propel their project to unprecedented heights.

But bridging the gap between strategy and execution demanded more than visionary thinking—it demanded meticulous planning and a meticulous eye for detail. Raj scrutinized timelines with the precision of a surgeon, identifying critical milestones and allocating resources with surgical precision. Each decision, each pivot, was a calculated step towards the summit they aimed to conquer.

As weeks melted into months, Raj and his team encountered the inevitable trials that punctuate every ambitious endeavor. Scope crept, deadlines loomed, and setbacks threatened to derail their meticulously laid plans. Yet, in the crucible of adversity, Raj's leadership shone like a beacon. He rallied his team with unwavering optimism and a resolve that bordered on unyielding.

They recalibrated strategies, realigned priorities, and leveraged setbacks as springboards for innovation. Communication became their lifeblood, fostering a culture of transparency and collaboration that transcended hierarchies. Through late nights and early mornings, through moments of doubt and fleeting triumphs, Raj steered their ship through turbulent waters with the steady hand of a seasoned captain.

And then, on a crisp autumn morning when the city awoke to the promise of a new day, Raj and his team stood atop the summit they had tirelessly ascended. The project—a testament to their collective resilience and unwavering commitment—gleamed like a jewel amidst the skyline. Stakeholders applauded, accolades poured in, and whispers of their success echoed through the corridors of industry.

But for Raj, the true measure of success lay not in accolades but in the transformative impact their project wielded. From strategy to action, they had bridged the chasm that often separates vision from reality. They had not just delivered a project—they had laid the foundation for future innovations and breakthroughs.

In the quietude of reflection, as Raj sipped his chai on the balcony overlooking the city he called home, he contemplated the journey that had led him here. Strategic planning and meticulous execution had been their lodestar, guiding them through the labyrinth of challenges and uncertainties. But it was the camaraderie forged in the crucible of adversity and the relentless pursuit of excellence that defined their success.

As he watched the sun dip below the horizon, casting a golden glow upon the skyline, Raj smiled. For in the crucible of strategic planning and execution, he had discovered not just the keys to project management success, but the enduring power of teamwork, resilience, and unwavering dedication to a shared vision. And in that realization, he found solace knowing that the journey from strategy to action had not just transformed projects—it had transformed lives.

key Points: -

1. **Context and Challenge**:

➤ Raj, a seasoned project manager in Mumbai, faced a high-stakes project set to redefine standards.

➤ His experience prepared him for navigating complex timelines and uncertainties inherent in such endeavors.

2. **Strategic Blueprint**:

➤ Raj's approach emphasized precision and foresight, crafting a blueprint for success that prioritized collaboration and excellence.

➤ The boardroom presentations were complemented by a deep commitment to translating plans into actionable steps.

3. **Execution Challenges**:

➤ Moving from strategy to execution revealed unforeseen obstacles and the gritty reality of implementation.

> Raj viewed strategic planning as a continuous compass guiding decisions and actions amid complexities.

4. **Team Dynamics:**

> With a diverse team, Raj fostered a culture of innovation through rigorous meetings where ideas converged into actionable strategies.

> He emphasized clarity of purpose and unwavering determination as foundational to their journey.

5. **Meticulous Planning:**

> Raj meticulously scrutinized timelines, identified critical milestones, and allocated resources with precision akin to surgical planning.

> Each decision and adjustment aimed to propel the project towards its ambitious goals.

6. **Leadership Amid Adversity:**

> Adversity tested the team with scope changes, looming deadlines, and setbacks, but Raj's leadership remained steadfast.

> He inspired optimism, resilience, and adaptive thinking, leveraging setbacks for innovative breakthroughs.

7. **Achievement and Impact**:

➤ Despite challenges, Raj and his team reached the summit of their project, earning industry acclaim and stakeholder recognition.

➤ Their success was measured not just in accolades but in the transformative impact their project had on the industry.

8. **Reflection and Lessons**:

➤ Reflecting on their journey, Raj found that strategic planning and meticulous execution were fundamental to their success.

➤ Beyond project management, he valued the camaraderie, resilience, and dedication to shared goals that defined their achievement.

9. **Legacy and Future**:

➤ Raj's story concludes with a realization of the enduring power of teamwork and dedication to a shared vision.

➤ Their journey from strategy to action not only transformed projects but also impacted lives, leaving a legacy of excellence and innovation.

Chapter 6.

The Art of Communication

6.(a)

Crisis Management

The Art of Resilience

In the gleaming glass towers of Manhattan, where ambition and innovation danced a delicate tango, Jessica stood at the helm of a thriving tech empire. As CEO, she had steered her company through turbulent seas, navigating market fluctuations and technological upheavals with finesse. But nothing could have prepared her for the storm that loomed on the horizon—a PR crisis that threatened to unravel years of painstaking brand building.

It began with a whisper—a leaked memo that cast shadows on the company's commitment to customer privacy. Within hours, the whisper crescendoed into a cacophony of outrage on social media platforms and headlines that screamed betrayal. Panic gripped boardrooms, and uncertainty cast a pall over once-confident executive.

For Jessica, crisis management was not merely a checklist of damage control measures—it was an art form that demanded clarity of vision and unwavering resolve. With steely composure, she convened her crisis management team—a cadre of seasoned advisors and communicators who had weathered storms of similar magnitude. Transparent communication became their North Star, illuminating the path through the tempest.

In a series of carefully orchestrated statements and press releases, Jessica acknowledged the gravity of the situation with humility and contrition. She pledged transparency and accountability, inviting stakeholders into the fold of decision-making. Behind closed doors, strategic planning sessions unfolded like a chess match, each move calculated to rebuild trust and fortify the company's battered reputation.

As the crisis unfurled its tendrils across the global marketplace, Jessica rallied her workforce with unwavering resolve. Town hall meetings became forums for candid dialogue, where employees voiced concerns and rallied behind a shared commitment to emerge stronger. Morale teetered on a knife's edge, but Jessica's leadership imbued the company with a sense of purpose that transcended adversity.

Outside the confines of boardrooms and office suites, Jessica engaged directly with customers and stakeholders. Town halls became virtual platforms for listening and learning, where she absorbed feedback with humility and charted a path forward with unyielding determination. Amidst the chaos, a semblance of order emerged—a testament to the transformative power of effective crisis management.

Weeks turned into months as Jessica and her team navigated the labyrinthine aftermath of the PR crisis. Gradually, skepticism yielded to cautious optimism, as stakeholders witnessed tangible strides towards redemption. New policies safeguarded customer privacy with unprecedented rigor, while investments in transparency initiatives forged stronger bonds of trust.

And then, on a crisp spring morning when the city bloomed with the promise of renewal, Jessica stood before a gathering of industry leaders and stakeholders. Her voice, once tinged with uncertainty, resonated with unwavering conviction as she recounted the journey from crisis to catharsis. The company, she declared, had emerged not just intact but strengthened by the crucible of adversity.

In the quietude of reflection, as Jessica gazed out over the city skyline aglow with the hues of sunset, she pondered the lessons gleaned from the crucible of crisis management. Effective crisis management, she realized, transcended mere strategy—it was a testament to resilience, integrity, and the transformative power of transparent communication.

As she sipped her coffee, Jessica contemplated the future with a renewed sense of purpose. The PR crisis had tested her mettle as a leader and reshaped her company's trajectory in ways unforeseen. Yet, amidst the chaos, she had discovered the enduring truth that in every crisis lay the seeds of opportunity for renewal and redemption.

And as the city lights twinkled like stars in the gathering dusk, Jessica smiled—a quiet affirmation that in the art of resilience, she had found not just survival, but the blueprint for enduring success.

key Points: -

1. **Initial Impact of Crisis**: A leaked memo triggered a PR crisis, threatening the company's reputation built over years.

2. **Leadership Response**: Jessica, the CEO, saw crisis management as an art requiring clear vision and unwavering resolve.

3. **Team Engagement**: She assembled a crisis management team of seasoned advisors and communicators to navigate the storm.

4. **Communication Strategy**: Transparent communication became central, addressing concerns with humility and pledging accountability.

5. **Internal Morale**: Town hall meetings boosted morale and solidarity among employees, emphasizing a shared commitment to recovery.

6. **External Stakeholder Engagement**: Jessica engaged directly with customers and stakeholders, using feedback to shape recovery efforts.

7. **Strategic Recovery**: Over months, strategic planning and policy changes rebuilt trust and strengthened customer privacy measures.

8. **Public Declaration**: Jessica publicly acknowledged the journey from crisis to renewal, showcasing the company's resilience and lessons learned.

9. **Personal Growth**: The crisis tested Jessica's leadership but also revealed the transformative power of resilience and integrity.

10. **Outcome**: The company emerged stronger, demonstrating that effective crisis management is not just about survival but also about seizing opportunities for growth and renewal.

6.(b)

Resilience and Recovery

The Rebuilding Entrepreneur

Mark was known around town as the tireless owner of a small but beloved bookstore, nestled in the heart of Maplewood. His shop, "Pages & Prose," was not just a place to buy books but a community hub where bookworms, students, and families gathered for literary discussions, author readings, and coffee-fueled conversations.

Mark had poured his heart and soul into building this business from scratch. It wasn't always easy, but his passion for books and his dedication to his customers kept him going through the ups and downs. He knew every corner of his shop intimately—the creaky wooden floors, the shelves filled with stories waiting to be discovered, and the cozy reading nook by the window where the sunlight streamed in every morning.

Little did Mark know that soon everything he had built would face its greatest test.

It was a warm summer afternoon when the weather suddenly took a turn. The sky darkened ominously, and the wind began to howl through the streets of Maplewood. Mark watched anxiously as the storm clouds gathered, feeling a knot of unease tighten in his stomach.

The local news warned of an approaching hurricane—a rare occurrence in their usually tranquil town. Residents hurried to secure their homes and businesses, bracing themselves for what was to come.

Mark spent the evening boarding up windows and moving his most valuable books to higher shelves. He had insurance, of course, but his real concern was for the heart of his business— the community that relied on Pages & Prose for more than just books.

As night fell, the hurricane made landfall with a ferocity that shook the town to its core. Rain lashed against the bookstore windows, and the wind roared like a freight train. Mark stayed up all night, listening to the sounds of destruction outside, praying that his beloved shop would withstand the onslaught.

When dawn finally broke, Maplewood emerged battered and bruised. Streets were flooded, trees were uprooted, and buildings lay in ruins. Mark's heart sank as he surveyed the damage. Pages & Prose had not escaped unscathed—the roof had partially collapsed, and water had seeped in, damaging countless books and furnishings.

But amidst the devastation, Mark found a glimmer of hope. The community rallied around him, offering help in any way they could. Neighbors, customers, and even strangers showed up with tools, supplies, and unwavering support.

The days that followed were a blur of hard work and determination. With the help of volunteers and friends, Mark began the daunting task of cleaning up and rebuilding. Every morning at dawn, they would gather outside Pages & Prose, armed with brooms, buckets, and a shared sense of purpose.

It wasn't easy. There were moments of frustration and exhaustion, times when it seemed like the damage was too much to overcome. But Mark refused to give up. He drew strength from the resilience of his community and the unwavering support of his loyal customers.

Together, they transformed Pages & Prose from a disaster zone into a symbol of hope and renewal. They patched up the roof, replaced damaged shelves, and salvaged as many books as they could. The bookstore reopened its doors sooner than anyone had expected, thanks to the tireless efforts of Mark and his team.

As Mark welcomed customers back into Pages & Prose, he knew that things could never go back to exactly how they were before. The storm had changed him, changed his business. He embraced this change with a spirit of innovation and resilience.

Mark launched a series of events to celebrate the bookstore's reopening—a weekend-long literary festival featuring local authors, book signings, and children's storytelling sessions. He introduced a new online ordering system and expanded the café menu to attract more foot traffic.

Through it all, Mark remained committed to his community. He hosted fundraisers for local disaster relief efforts, donated books to schools and libraries, and became a vocal advocate for disaster preparedness.

Pages & Prose emerged from the storm stronger than ever, a testament to the power of resilience and community support. Mark's experience taught him valuable lessons about building organizational resilience—not just for his business but for himself and his team.

He implemented backup plans and disaster recovery protocols, ensuring that Pages & Prose would be better prepared for future challenges. He fostered a culture of open communication and collaboration among his staff, empowering them to take initiative and adapt to changing circumstances.

Through it all, Mark never forgot the kindness and generosity that had carried him through the darkest days. He remained deeply grateful to his community and committed to giving back in any way he could.

Years later, Pages & Prose continued to thrive. It had become more than just a bookstore—it was a symbol of resilience, hope, and the enduring power of community. Mark often found himself reflecting on the journey that had led him here—the storm that had tested him and the rebuilding process that had transformed him.

As he stood behind the counter one quiet afternoon, watching customers browse the shelves and children giggle in the reading nook, Mark felt a profound sense of gratitude. He had faced adversity head-on and emerged stronger on the other side. And though he knew there would always be challenges ahead, he also knew that with resilience, innovation, and the support of his community, there was nothing he couldn't overcome.

The Journey of Mark and his Resilient Business captured not just the story of one small bookstore but the universal tale of human resilience in the face of adversity. It reminded us that storms may shake our foundations, but they can also reveal the strength and spirit within us to rebuild, stronger and more determined than ever before.

key Points: -

1. **Initial Challenges and Dedication**: Mark built "Pages & Prose" from scratch, pouring his heart into creating a beloved community bookstore known for literary events and a welcoming atmosphere.

2. **The Storm Strikes**: A rare hurricane hits Maplewood, threatening Mark's bookstore and the community it serves. Despite preparations, the bookstore suffers damage, including a collapsed roof and water damage to books and furnishings.

3. **Community Support**: In the aftermath, Mark experiences an outpouring of support from the community. Neighbors, customers, and strangers come together to help clean up and rebuild, demonstrating the power of community solidarity in times of crisis.

4. **Resilience and Rebuilding**: Mark and his team embark on the challenging task of rebuilding. Despite setbacks and exhaustion, they persevere, drawing strength from each other and their shared determination to restore Pages & Prose.

5. **Innovation and Adaptation**: Post-recovery, Mark embraces change and innovation. He launches new initiatives such as a literary festival, an online ordering system, and an expanded café menu to rejuvenate the business and attract more customers.

6. **Organizational Resilience**: Mark implements disaster recovery plans and fosters a resilient culture within his business. He prioritizes communication, collaboration, and preparedness to ensure Pages & Prose can withstand future challenges.

7. **Community Engagement**: Mark remains deeply connected to his community, organizing fundraisers, donating books, and advocating for disaster preparedness. This ongoing commitment reinforces the bookstore's role as a community pillar.

8. **Reflection and Gratitude**: Years later, Pages & Prose thrives as a symbol of resilience and community spirit.

Mark reflects on his journey, acknowledging the lessons learned and expressing gratitude for the support that helped him rebuild stronger than before.

9. **Universal Themes**: Mark's story illustrates universal themes of resilience, hope, and the transformative power of community support in overcoming adversity. It serves as a reminder that while challenges may test us, they can also reveal our inner strength and capacity for growth.

10. **Inspiration and Motivation**: Mark's journey inspires others facing adversity to persevere with resilience, innovation, and the support of their communities, showing that even after storms, there is always potential for renewal and growth.

Chapter 7.

The Art of Communication

Sustainable Business Practice

The Green Manufacturer

In the foothills of the Sierra Nevada, nestled among towering pine trees and crystal-clear streams, stood the headquarters of Patagonia Manufacturing. Founded decades ago by environmentalist Yvon Chouinard, the company had humble beginnings as a small outdoor gear workshop. Over the years, it had grown into a global icon known for its commitment to environmental sustainability.

At the heart of Patagonia's ethos was a deep reverence for nature. Yvon believed that businesses had a responsibility not just to make profits but to minimize their environmental footprint and contribute positively to the planet. This philosophy shaped every decision made within the company—from sourcing materials to manufacturing processes.

The turning point came in the early 2000s when a series of environmental reports highlighted the devastating impact of industrial manufacturing on the planet. Yvon, already attuned to these issues, gathered his team and made a bold declaration: Patagonia would lead the charge in sustainable business practices, setting a new standard for the industry.

They began by scrutinizing every aspect of their supply chain. From the organic cotton used in their clothing to the recycled materials in their backpacks, every decision was guided by a commitment to environmental stewardship. It wasn't just about compliance—it was about going above and beyond to protect the planet they loved.

Implementing sustainable practices wasn't easy. It required innovation, investment, and a willingness to challenge the status quo. Patagonia's engineers and designers worked tirelessly to develop new techniques and materials that minimized waste and reduced energy consumption.

They pioneered the use of recycled polyester in their outerwear, created a revolutionary waterless dyeing process for their fabrics, and partnered with suppliers who shared their commitment to fair labor practices and environmental responsibility.

The journey was fraught with challenges and setbacks. There were skeptics who doubted the feasibility of their ambitious goals and competitors who scoffed at their unconventional methods. But Yvon and his team remained steadfast, driven by their conviction that sustainability was not just a trend but a fundamental principle of good business.

As Patagonia's commitment to sustainability became widely known, the company began to influence industry practices on a global scale. They published their environmental footprint openly, inspiring transparency and accountability among their peers. Other companies started to emulate Patagonia's approach, realizing that sustainability wasn't just a moral imperative but a competitive advantage in a changing world.

Patagonia's influence extended beyond their own operations. They partnered with environmental organizations, lobbied for policy changes that promoted sustainability, and engaged with consumers to raise awareness about the importance of making conscious purchasing decisions.

Despite their success, Patagonia faced numerous challenges along the way. Economic pressures, fluctuating market demands, and the complexities of global supply chains tested their resolve. Yet, each challenge served as an opportunity to innovate and strengthen their commitment to sustainability.

During a global economic downturn, instead of compromising on their values, Patagonia doubled down on their efforts. They launched repair and reuse programs, encouraging customers to extend the life of their products rather than discard them. They invested in renewable energy sources for their facilities and continued to refine their manufacturing processes to minimize waste.

By integrating sustainability into every facet of their business strategy, Patagonia not only survived but thrived. Their dedication to environmental stewardship became a cornerstone of their brand identity, attracting a loyal customer base who shared their values. Employees were proud to work for a company that prioritized planet over profit, fostering a culture of innovation and responsibility.

As Patagonia looked towards the future, they remained committed to pushing the boundaries of what was possible. They set ambitious goals to further reduce their carbon footprint, protect endangered ecosystems, and advocate for policies that promoted environmental conservation.

Today, Patagonia stands as a testament to the power of sustainable business practices. From their humble beginnings in a small workshop to their position as a global leader in outdoor gear, they have proven that profitability and environmental responsibility can go hand in hand.

Yvon Chouinard's vision continues to guide Patagonia forward, inspiring countless businesses to rethink their approach to sustainability. As the world faces unprecedented environmental challenges, Patagonia remains a beacon of hope—a reminder that through innovation, dedication, and a deep respect for nature, we can build a future where business thrives without compromising the planet.

key Points: -

1. **Founding Principles**: Founded by Yvon Chouinard, Patagonia Manufacturing began with a strong commitment to environmental sustainability and a deep reverence for nature.

2. **Commitment to Sustainability**: Patagonia believes businesses should minimize their environmental footprint and contribute positively to the planet, not just focus on profits.

3. **Leadership in Sustainability**: In the early 2000s, Patagonia decided to lead in sustainable business practices after reports highlighted the negative impact of industrial manufacturing on the environment.

4. **Comprehensive Approach**: Patagonia scrutinized every part of their supply chain, from sourcing organic materials like cotton to using recycled materials in products like backpacks.

5. **Innovative Practices**: They developed innovative techniques such as using recycled polyester and waterless dyeing processes to reduce waste and energy consumption.

6. **Industry Influence**: Patagonia's practices influenced global industry standards, encouraging transparency, accountability, and sustainability among peers.

7. **Beyond Operations**: Patagonia engaged in partnerships with environmental organizations, advocated for policy

changes, and educated consumers on conscious purchasing decisions.

8. **Challenges and Resilience**: Despite economic pressures and global challenges, Patagonia remained steadfast in its commitment to sustainability, doubling down on efforts during economic downturns.

9. **Integrated Sustainability**: Sustainability became a cornerstone of Patagonia's brand identity, attracting loyal customers and fostering a culture of innovation and responsibility among employees.

10. **Future Goals**: Patagonia continues to set ambitious goals to further reduce their carbon footprint, protect ecosystems, and advocate for environmental conservation.

11. **Inspiration and Legacy**: Yvon Chouinard's vision continues to inspire businesses to prioritize sustainability, demonstrating that profitability and environmental responsibility can coexist.

12. **Global Impact**: From a small workshop to a global leader, Patagonia proves that sustainable business practices can lead to long-term success while protecting the planet.

7.(b)

Corporate Social Responsibility

The Community Corporation

In the picturesque town of Burlington, nestled between the rolling hills of Vermont, lay the headquarters of Ben & Jerry's, more than just an ice cream company, but a beacon of Corporate Social Responsibility (CSR). Founded by two friends, Ben Cohen and Jerry Greenfield, their journey began with a simple dream: to make the world's best ice cream, in the best possible way.

Ben and Jerry were not your typical corporate founders. They were guided not only by the desire for profit but also by a deep commitment to their community and the environment. As their business flourished, they realized that their success was intertwined with the well-being of those around them. This realization led them to pioneer innovative CSR initiatives long before it became a buzzword in boardrooms.

Their first initiative involved sourcing ingredients locally, supporting family farms, and ensuring fair wages for farmers. This decision not only improved the quality of their ice cream but also created a ripple effect of economic stability in the region. The community embraced Ben & Jerry's not just as a brand but as a partner in their prosperity.

As Ben & Jerry's grew, so did their responsibility. They faced the challenge of scaling their business while staying true to their values. This meant making tough decisions, such as refusing to use artificial growth hormones in their dairy products or sourcing cocoa from Fairtrade-certified cooperatives.

Their commitment to social and environmental causes became the cornerstone of their brand identity. Customers weren't just buying ice cream; they were supporting a movement for positive change. This authenticity earned them a loyal following and transformed Ben & Jerry's into a beloved household name.

Beyond their products, Ben & Jerry's ventured into advocacy and activism. They used their platform to raise awareness about climate change, social justice issues, and the importance of civic engagement. From partnering with NGOs to fund grassroots projects to advocating for policy changes, Ben & Jerry's became a force for good in the corporate world.

Their employees were not just staff members; they were ambassadors of their values. The company encouraged volunteerism and provided paid time off for employees to engage in community service. This culture of caring created a motivated workforce dedicated to making a difference.

Despite their successes, Ben & Jerry's faced criticisms from skeptics who questioned the feasibility of combining profitability with social responsibility. Some investors worried that their commitment to higher wages and sustainable practices would compromise profits. However, Ben & Jerry's remained steadfast in their belief that doing good was not just the right thing to do but also good for business in the long run.

They navigated these challenges with transparency and humility, acknowledging that they weren't perfect but were always striving to improve. This openness earned them respect and credibility, even from their critics.

As Ben and Jerry approached retirement age, they began to plan for the future of their company and its legacy. They wanted to ensure that their commitment to CSR would endure beyond their tenure. They established a foundation dedicated to supporting social causes and empowering the next generation of changemakers.

Their successors embraced this vision, continuing to innovate and advocate for progressive values. Ben & Jerry's became a model for other companies looking to balance profit with social and environmental responsibilities. Their impact extended far beyond the confines of their headquarters in Vermont, inspiring a global movement towards conscious capitalism.

Today, Ben & Jerry's stands as a testament to the power of Corporate Social Responsibility. Their journey proves that a company can achieve both profitability and positive social impact by prioritizing people and planet alongside profit. As they continue to expand their reach and influence, they remain committed to their founding principles of peace, love, and ice cream.

key Points: -

1. **Founding Principles**: Ben Cohen and Jerry Greenfield founded Ben & Jerry's with a strong commitment not only to making quality ice cream but also to contributing positively to their community and the environment.

2. **Local Sourcing and Fair Practices**: They pioneered CSR initiatives early on by sourcing ingredients locally, supporting family farms, and ensuring fair wages for farmers. This initiative aimed to enhance product quality and contribute to local economic stability.

3. **Values-Driven Business Growth**: As Ben & Jerry's grew, they faced challenges in scaling while maintaining their values. They made decisions like refusing to use artificial growth hormones and sourcing Fairtrade-certified cocoa, aligning with their commitment to social and environmental causes.

4. **Brand Identity and Customer Loyalty**: Their dedication to CSR became central to their brand identity, attracting customers who saw purchasing Ben & Jerry's products as supporting a movement for positive change.

5. **Advocacy and Activism**: Beyond product sales, Ben & Jerry's engaged in advocacy on climate change, social justice, and civic engagement. They partnered with NGOs,

funded grassroots projects, and advocated for policy changes, establishing themselves as a socially responsible corporate leader.

6. **Employee Engagement**: Ben & Jerry's fostered a culture where employees were encouraged to volunteer, with paid time off for community service. This approach cultivated a motivated workforce aligned with the company's values.

7. **Navigating Challenges**: Despite skepticism from critics about profitability versus social responsibility, Ben & Jerry's remained committed to their belief that doing good was not only ethical but also beneficial for long-term business success.

8. **Transparency and Accountability**: The company maintained transparency about their challenges and areas for improvement, earning respect and credibility even from critics.

9. **Legacy and Future Planning**: As Ben and Jerry approached retirement, they ensured the continuity of their CSR commitment by establishing a foundation supporting social causes and empowering future generations of changemakers.

10. **Global Influence**: Ben & Jerry's became a model for other companies seeking to balance profit with social and environmental responsibilities, sparking a global movement towards conscious capitalism.

11. **Core Values**: Their journey exemplifies that profitability can coexist with positive social impact when a company prioritizes values like peace, love, and responsible business practices.

12. **Ongoing Commitment**: Today, Ben & Jerry's continues to expand their influence while remaining true to their founding principles of CSR, demonstrating that sustained commitment to social responsibility can lead to enduring business success.

Conclusion

The Future of Management Tantra

Envisioning the Future

The Integrated Leader

In the heart of a bustling city, amidst the towering skyscrapers and bustling streets, Lily stood at the helm of her company, a beacon of innovation and resilience. She wasn't just a leader; she was an advocate for a new way of managing organizations — one that integrated ancient wisdom with modern practices.

Lily's journey began with a simple yet profound realization: that the future of management lay not in rigid hierarchies and profit-driven decisions but in embracing holistic principles that nurtured both people and performance. She delved into the teachings of Management Tantra, a philosophy that emphasized balance, mindfulness, and interconnectedness in leadership.

Under Lily's leadership, the organization underwent a transformation. She introduced practices inspired by Management Tantra: fostering a culture of trust and transparency, encouraging open communication across all levels, and prioritizing the well-being of employees as much as the bottom line.

Teams became more cohesive, fueled by a shared sense of purpose and empowered to innovate. Lily understood that resilience came not just from robust strategies but from a workforce that felt valued and heard. She implemented flexible work policies, supported mental health initiatives, and championed diversity and inclusion.

Lily faced challenges along the way. Skeptics questioned the efficacy of her approach, arguing that traditional management methods were tried and tested. Yet, Lily persisted, guided by her belief that embracing change and adapting to the evolving needs of the workforce and society were crucial for long-term success.

During times of crisis, such as economic downturns or industry disruptions, Lily's organization proved its resilience. Teams rallied together, drawing strength from their shared values and collaborative spirit. They pivoted swiftly, innovating new products and services that met emerging market demands while staying true to their commitment to sustainability and social responsibility.

As word of Lily's success spread, other leaders began to take notice. Inspired by her example, they started integrating principles of Management Tantra into their own organizations. What began as a personal journey for Lily evolved into a movement towards a more enlightened approach to leadership and management.

Organizations that embraced these principles flourished, not only in terms of financial performance but also in employee satisfaction and community impact. They became role models in their industries, demonstrating that profitability and social responsibility were not mutually exclusive but complementary aspects of a thriving business.

Looking ahead, Lily saw a world where Management Tantra was not just a trend but a cornerstone of organizational philosophy. Leaders would continue to blend traditional wisdom with modern practices, creating workplaces that were not only efficient and productive but also compassionate and sustainable.

The future of management belonged to those who could navigate complexity with grace, who understood that true leadership meant fostering a sense of belonging and purpose among their teams. Lily envisioned a future where integrated leaders inspired innovation, embraced diversity, and spearheaded efforts towards a more equitable society.

Lily's legacy as an integrated leader endured long after her retirement. Her organization continued to thrive under the guidance of leaders who shared her vision. They expanded their impact globally, partnering with communities to tackle pressing social and environmental challenges while maintaining a profitable business model.

The principles of Management Tantra became ingrained in the fabric of organizations across industries, shaping a new paradigm of leadership that prioritized holistic growth and sustainable practices. Lily's journey had not only transformed her company but had also set a precedent for future generations of leaders to follow.

As the sun set on another successful day, Lily reflected on her journey with gratitude. She had not only led a thriving organization but had also paved the way for a brighter, more interconnected future of management, where wisdom from the past guided innovation for tomorrow.

Lily's story illustrates how integrating ancient wisdom with modern management practices can create resilient, innovative, and socially responsible organizations poised for the future. Her journey inspires us to envision leadership as a holistic endeavor that balances profitability with purpose, embracing change as a catalyst for growth and sustainability.

key Points:

1. **Introduction to Lily and Management Tantra:**

➢ Lily embodies a new breed of leader who integrates ancient wisdom with modern management practices.

➢ Management Tantra emphasizes balance, mindfulness, and interconnectedness in leadership.

2. **Transformation Under Lily's Leadership**:

   ➢ Lily's organization undergoes a profound transformation under her guidance.

   ➢ She introduces trust, transparency, and open communication, prioritizing employee well-being alongside business goals.

   ➢ Teams become more cohesive, purpose-driven, and innovative.

3. **Challenges and Resilience**:

   ➢ Despite skepticism, Lily persists in her belief that adaptive, holistic management is key to long-term success.

   ➢ During crises, her organization proves resilient, innovating and adapting swiftly while maintaining social responsibility.

4. **Impact and Spread of Management Tantra**:

   ➢ Lily's success inspires other leaders to adopt Management Tantra principles.

   ➢ Organizations embracing these principles thrive financially, enhance employee satisfaction, and make a positive community impact.

5. **Future Vision**:

➤ Management Tantra is envisioned as a foundational philosophy for future leaders.

➤ Integrated leaders will navigate complexity with grace, fostering belonging, purpose, and innovation.

6. **Legacy of Leadership**:

➤ Lily's legacy endures beyond her retirement as her organization continues to thrive globally.

➤ Management Tantra becomes integral across industries, shaping a new leadership paradigm focused on holistic growth and sustainability.

7. **Conclusion**:

➤ Lily's journey illustrates how integrating ancient wisdom with modern practices can create resilient, innovative, and socially responsible organizations.

➤ Her story encourages leaders to embrace a holistic approach that balances profitability with purpose, driving growth through innovation and sustainability.

Practical Tools and Exercises

Comprehensive Toolkit for

Professional Growth and Well-being

Mindfulness Exercises:

- **Breathing Techniques:** Simple exercises to practice mindful breathing for stress reduction and focus.

- **Body Scan Meditation:** Guided meditation to cultivate awareness of bodily sensations and promote relaxation.

Communication Templates:

- **Effective Feedback Framework:** A structured template for delivering constructive feedback to team members.

- **Conflict Resolution Script:** Step-by-step guide for navigating difficult conversations and resolving conflicts positively.

Strategic Planning Worksheets:

- **SWOT Analysis Worksheet:** Template for conducting a SWOT (Strengths, Weaknesses, Opportunities, Threats) analysis to assess organizational strategies.

- **Goal Setting Planner:** Tool to help define SMART (Specific, Measurable, Achievable, Relevant, Time-bound) goals and create action plans.

Team-Building Activities:

- **Team Vision Board Exercise:** Collaborative activity to visualize and align team goals and aspirations.

- **Strengths Assessment:** Tool to identify individual strengths within the team and leverage them for improved collaboration.

Personal Development Exercises:

- **Reflective Journal Prompts:** Thought-provoking prompts to encourage self-reflection and personal growth.

- **Career Development Plan Template:** Framework for setting career goals and mapping out professional development steps.

Wellness and Self-Care Tools:

- **Daily Self-Care Checklist:** Checklist to promote self-care habits and well-being in daily routines.

- **Stress Management Techniques:** Strategies and exercises for managing stress effectively in the workplace.

Notes

www.ingramcontent.com/pod-product-compliance
Lightning Source LLC
Chambersburg PA
CBHW061734020426
42331CB00006B/1239